Further Genealogical Notes on the Tyrrell-Terrell Family

of Virginia and Its English and Norman-French Progenitors

By Edwin Holland Terrell

PANTIANOS
CLASSICS

Published by Pantianos Classics

ISBN-13: 978-1-78987-553-9

First published in 1909

Contents

Dedication

To the memory of My Brother,

𝔊eneral 𝔠harles 𝔐ilton 𝔗errell,

U. S. Army,

Who took an Absorbing Interest in the Ancient History
of his Family, this Little Pamphlet is Affectionately Dedicated.

The Ancient Heraldic Arms and Crest

of the
Tyrrells of Heron, from whom the
Tyrrells of Springfield and the Tyrrells of Thornton,
from whom William Tyrrell (or Terrell)
of Virginia.

Arms: *Argent, within a bordure engrailed, gules, two chevrons, azure.*

Crest: *A peacock's tail issuing from the mouth of a boar's head, couped, erect.*

Supporters: *Two tigers, regardant.*

Motto: *Sans Dieu Rien. (Without God, Nothing).*

Preface

In 1907, the author of this little pamphlet published a preliminary sketch of the ancient history of what he called the Tyrrell and Terrell family of Virginia. He had recently returned from a trip abroad, during which he spent some little time in London, where he made some researches in the library of the British Museum on the subject of the early history of this well-known Virginia family. He did not have the time to make any very extensive investigations into the subject, and was obliged to rely very largely for the data, upon which was based the sketch he subsequently prepared on his return home, upon a very eminent authority he found in this great library, called in French, "Histoire Généalogique et Héraldique de la Maison des Tyrel, Sires, puis Princes de Poix, et des Familles de Moyencourt et de Poix."

Some time after the issue of the little pamphlet above referred to, the author learned of the publication in England in 1904 of a very authentic and complete history of the Tyrrell family, compiled by Joseph Henry Tyrrell, of "Castleknock," Queen's Road, Twickenham, England. This book was sent for and was found to be one of the most thoroughly prepared genealogical histories of a family ever issued. Correspondence was at once opened with Mr. Tyrrell, the English author of this book, and as a result of this correspondence, which has gone on now for over a year, and from a careful study of the pedigrees contained in this English history of the family, the author of this little pamphlet has deemed it expedient to issue a second edition, in order to correct many errors which were found to exist in his first edition and to make many important additions which he first learned of through the more elaborate history above referred to. During the correspondence with Mr. Tyrrell, the English historian of the family, he very kindly annotated with valuable notes the pamphlet which had been published by the author in 1907, making many little corrections in the historical data, and many valuable suggestions as to important facts hitherto unknown by the author. In the following pages no attempt will be made to give anything but a brief resumé of the exceedingly interesting matter contained in this rare history prepared in England; it is recommended, however, that those members of the family who are desirous of making more elaborate researches into the history of this old family should send to Mr. Tyrrell and obtain a copy of his book while the limited edition of it lasts. Only one hundred copies were published, and while any of the edition lasts it can be obtained by sending two pounds, four shillings to Mr. Tyrrell at the address given above.

EDWIN HOLLAND TERRELL.

"Lambermont,"
San Antonio, Texas,
    March, 1909.

The Tyrrell-Terrell Family

The founder of this family, known as *de Tirel, Tirel, Tyrel, Tyrell, Tyrrell, Terrell, Tirrell,* (and with other variations in the orthography), was *Ralf, Sire de Tirel, de Poix and de Guernanville,* son of *Walter I., Count of the Vexin and Amiens.*

The Counts of the Vexin were the lords of a district situated on the northern borders of France as they existed in the tenth century and which lay between France and the ducal possessions of the House of Normandy. This little district, known as the Vexin, was sometimes under the suzerain control of the Norman dukes and sometimes under that of the French crown; but finally became absorbed with Normandy by the latter. The father of *Ralf de Tirel, Walter I., Count of the Vexin,* lived about 995 and was lord proprietor over many lands even beyond the Vexin. He was the son of *Waleran, Count of the Vexin,* and hereditary standard bearer of France, who died in 965. The mother of Walter I., was *Edelgarde,* a daughter of the *Count of Flanders* and a great-granddaughter of *Alfred the Great of England.* Walter I. was also lineally descended from *Pepin le Gros, Charles Martel, Duke of Brabant,* and *Charlemagne.* He was also lineally descended from the Dukes of Burgundy. These pedigrees, with the marriages, from Pepin le Gros, Charles Martel and Charlemagne to Ralf de Tirel are given in Mr. Tyrrell's history of the family. Walter I. married *Eve,* daughter and heiress of *Landry, Count of Dreux.* Ralf de Tirel was the fourth son of this marriage. Ralf, the first to bear the name of Tirel, had his castle near the village of *Tirel* on the banks of the Seine, a short distance below Paris, from which he took the surname of *Tirel.* Having married a daughter of the *Seigneur of Guernanville,* he became in time the *Seigneur of Guernanville,* the *Chatelain of Pontoise* and the *Viscount of Amiens.* The little village of Tirel on the banks of the Seine is now known in modern orthography as Triel, a mere transposition of two letters. The ancient spelling of the village name was Tirel.

From the time of its founder, Ralf, the family name has been spelled in many different ways, depending on the language in which it was spelled and probably on the changing taste of its different members in a matter of this kind. In the old Norman histories, such as Ordericus Vitalis and others, it appears in several different ways, such as *Tirel, Tyrell, Tyrrell, etc.* In one of the alumni registers of the University of Oxford in England, containing the graduates of that old university between 1571 and 1622, Volume II., on page 413, the following various spellings are given of the family name as constituting one and the same family, viz., *Tirrell, Terill, Terrell, Terrill, Tirrill, Tyrell* and *Tyrrell.* The commonly accepted spelling of the family name in England for the past four hundred years has been *Tyrrell.* In the old colonial land records at Richmond, Virginia, where the first mention is made of the Virginia ancestor of the family, the name of *William Terrell* is spelled *William Tyrrell;* and the name of his brother, *Richmond Terrell,* is spelled in the same early records *Richmond Tirrell.* In many parts of Virginia still, and in some other states where branches of the same family are established, the name is still pronounced as though it were spelled *Tirrell.*

When the author of this pamphlet was the American Envoy and Minister at Brussels, (1889-1893), his British colleague was Lord Vivian, a nobleman of most distinguished ancestry in England. Lord Vivian always called him Mr. "Tirrell." On the author's explaining to him one day that his name was spelled "Terrell" and was pronounced as that name is usually pronounced in America, Lord Vivian replied, "Your name is that of one of the oldest County families in England and the name is spelled in English history in various ways, but it is always pronounced as though it were spelled 'Tirrell,' and in England, even if the name should be written 'Terrell' it would be pronounced 'Tirrell.'" While the author was making his researches in the British Museum library he was always addressed by the officers and attendants about the library as Mr. "Tirrell," although they had his card in their hand on which his name was engraved "Terrell." In the French book referred to in the preface to this little pamphlet the family name is given as *"Tyrrell de Poix,"* and in the frequent references to the family in that history it is always spoken of in that way when the family name is mentioned. This addition of the affix *"de Poix"* came from the fact that among the many titles possessed by *Ralf* and his descendants was that of *Lord of Poix,* and ultimately *Prince of Poix.* The village of Poix is situated 26 kilometres southwest of Amiens and 116 kilometres north of Paris, on the railroad line from Paris to Calais, and on the line from Amiens to Rouen. (The name of this little village should be pronounced "Po-ah," and not "Poy," nor "Poyicks").

This French history of the old Norman family found by the author of this pamphlet in the British Museum library was prepared by M. Cuvillier-Morel-D'Acy, a distinguished archivist and genealogist of France. The book was published at Paris by the author in 1869, and as the author states, the data for this elaborate history of this old Norman-French family came from manuscripts preserved for many centuries in the *Moyencourt* family, which was related to the *Tyrreil* family through descent and intermarriages. M. D'Acy says, "The ancient House of the *Tyrrells* came from Normandy and was an issue of the first dukes of Normandy and very old and distinguished. In the charter of the primal church of Rouen in 1030 *Walter Tyrrell* is mentioned, and is there stated to be a wealthy nobleman and a close kinsman or cousin of *Robert, Duke of Normandy.*" The Robert, Duke of Normandy, here mentioned is the one familiarly known as *Robert, the Magnificent,* and sometimes as *Robert the Devil,* fifth Duke of Normandy, who was the father of *William the Conqueror.* The English historian of the family, Mr. Tyrrell, gives the exact pedigrees of the family from Ralf, the founder, down to the present time. These pedigrees have evidently been prepared with great care and are based upon authorities easily accessible in England which Mr. Tyrrell regards as absolutely reliable. In fact, Mr. Tyrrell gives in his book a list of the authorities he has consulted in the preparation of his history, and they are, generally speaking, very rare and expensive books which it would be impossible for anyone on this side of the Atlantic to be able to consult. They include many old French and Norman family histories, books published by archaeological societies, County pedigrees, works on extinct titles, books on heraldry, and many of the earliest books published in the English language on genealogy. According to these pedigree lists, the second son of *Ralf, Viscount of Amiens,* was *Fulk de Tirel,* who became the *Seigneur of Guernanville* and *Dean of Evreux.* He married *Orielda,* who was a daughter of *Richard I.,* the third Duke of Normandy. Among the children of Fulk de Tirel and Orielda was Walter, known in history as *Sir Walter Tyrrell I., Lord of Poix, Castellan of Pontoise,* and a Baron of both France and England. This was the *Sir Walter Tyrrell* who accompanied his relative, *Duke William of Normandy, in* the expedition which led to the conquest of England, and who was present at the battle of Senlac or Hastings.

According to M. D'Acy's book, the House of Tyrrell was prominent both in Picardy and in Normandy. Its members made themselves distinguished for their rich seigneurial possessions and their high positions in this province and in the neighboring provinces of France. They were possessed of many fiefs. They were *Lords* and *Princes de Poix, de Brimen, Conty, Frémontiers, Morenil, and de Ribécourt.* They were *Viscomtes d'Equennes et de St. Maxent; Barons d'Angles et de Prunget* and lords of ninety-four towns in *Picardy, Brittany, Berry, Poitou, Touraine, Valois, Vermandois, etc.* The first member of the family to bear the title of Prince de Poix was Hugues, (in English, Hugh), who was a great-grandson of the first Sir Walter, and who will be hereafter spoken of. The Hugh Tyrrell who firmly established the Tyrrell family in England, was this *Hugh Tyrrell I., Prince de Poix.* The family in Picardy, in the male line, died out in 1417, and all its possessions and titles passed from those of that name to the illustrious House of *Moyencourt,* through a female member of the Tyrrell family, who had married a Moyencourt. When that family ceased to exist in the direct male line in 1510, the titles and possessions passed into the great family of de *Créquy,* also descendants, through marriage, of the Tyrrells. The book gives the direct descent of the possessions and titles as follows:

House of the Tyrrells, 1030-1417;

House of the Moyencourt and Soissons-Morenil families,

House of de Créquy, 1510-1574: 1417-1510;

House of Blanchefort-Créquy, 1574-1687;

House de la Tremoille, 1687-1717;

House de Rouillé, 1718-1729;

House de Noailles, 1729-

Many of the landed possessions in France of the old family of Tyrrell de Poix, and such of its titles as have not become extinct, are now held by *Francois Napoléon de Noailles, Duc de Mouchy* and *Prince de Poix,* a lineal descendant of the old Norman-Picardian family.

Sir Walter Tyrrell I., according to the English historian of the family, was both of Norman and French extraction, being a descendant of the Norman Dukes and at the same time a lineal descendant of the *Dukes of Burgundy and Brabant* and of the *House of Charlemagne.* He was the possessor of the lands of *Bussy, Croixrault, Equennes, Famechon, Frémontiers, Moyencourt, etc.* According to M. D'Acy, his descendants in England are represented by the well-known County family of *Tyrrell, Terrell* and *Tirrell,* established in Hampshire and Essex Counties by him and his descendants in the earlier years after the Conquest.

Sir Walter Tyrrell I. is represented now in France in descent by two principal branches: first, the *Moyencourt* family, and second, the *Mouchy de Poix* family. The family of *Tyrrell de Poix* figured prominently in the Crusades; they held high positions at the courts of the kings of France in the early days; produced a Grand Admiral of France, who was killed on the French side at the battle of Agincourt; were governors of cities; and filled many other positions of importance in the military and civil history of the north of France.

As before stated, *Walter Tyrrell I.* accompanied *William the Conqueror* to the conquest of England. Being a close kinsman, or cousin, as M. D'Acy's book calls it, of Duke William of Normandy,' he asked to have the honor of leading one of the columns in the first assault upon the English lines at the battle of Senlac (Hastings); he was accorded this honorable post, and with his large and well trained band of retainers from Poix he participated prominently in the assault on the English left wing at the great battle of October 14, 1066.

The name of *Tyrrell* is mentioned in the "Cartulaire de St. Martin de la Bataille," which was a list of the distinguished noblemen who took part in this great decisive battle. See also list published by André Duchesne for the name of *Gauthier Tyrrell*, it being understood that the French spelling of the English name of Walter is Gauthier. His name is also inscribed on the walls of the Church of Dives, at the little port of Normandy, put there in 1861 by one of the antiquarian societies of France. Duke William's army assembled for the Conquest at this little port of Dives.

In 1046, *Sir Walter Tyrrell I.* with *Alix,* his wife, built the Chateau de Poix et de Moyencourt, and also the fortress of Famechon, and he became one of the most powerful lords of the country and the stem of one of the most illustrious Houses that ever existed in Picardy. He married twice, first, a Saxon lady by the name of *Olga;* and second, *Alix, Dame de Frémontiers,* the only daughter of Richard, *Seigneur de Frémontiers.* He had by his first marriage a son, *Sir Walter Tyrrell II.* This son, Sir Walter Tyrrell II., died before his father, leaving a son, *Sir Walter Tyrrell III.* This Sir Walter Tyrrell III. is the member of the family who, it is said, accidentally killed King William Rufus of England, while hunting with him in New Forest. His name appears in several documents in Picardy as the grandson of Sir Walter Tyrrell I. Sir Walter Tyrrell I. died in 1068 or 1080, and was succeeded in his titles and possessions, both in England and

France, by his grandson Sir Walter III. The latter had accidentally killed the King, as aforesaid, August 2, 1100; he died at one of his chateaux in Picardy in 1135, after having made a journey to the Holy Land. The full account of the manner of the death of King William Rufus will be found in Augustin Thierry's History of France, and it will be found on examination to be full of most interesting details. In a recent letter to a kinsman of the author of this pamphlet, Lieutenant-General Frank Tyrrell, a retired officer of the English army, in speaking of the accidental killing of King William Rufus, refers to the tradition that Sir Walter Tyrrell III., after the accident, crossed the river Avon on his way to the coast at a ford which is still called Tyrrellsford. The scene of all this is in Hampshire, where the first lands that were granted to Sir Walter I. by William the Conqueror were located and where the village of Avon-Tyrrell still exists. In his letter General Tyrrell further says that the forge in a neighboring village is still shown where Sir Walter got the shoes on his horse's feet reversed in order to baffle pursuit. He also says that the Avon-Tyrrell property which belonged for so many generations to the Tyrrell family now belongs to Lord Manners.

Sir Walter Tyrrell III. married, by order of his kinsman, William the Conqueror, *Adelaide Giffard,* who was of the illustrious House of Giffard in Normandy and England, and who was the granddaughter of *Walter Giffard, first Earl of Buckingham,* and daughter of *Richard Giffard,* one of the lords of the court of the King of England, and of his wife *Mathilde de Mortemer,* daughter of *Walter de Mortemer,* in Normandy.

Sir Walter Tyrrell III. left, by Adelaide, his wife, a son, *Hugh Tyrrell I.* Sir Walter Tyrrell III. bore all the titles of his grandfather. *Lord of Poix, Vicomte d'Equennes, Baron de Ribécourt, etc.* He was a rich and powerful nobleman, owning vast possessions in Normandy, Picardy, Ponthieu, etc. He founded the Priory of St. Denis de Poix, in 1116, with the consent of his wife and his son Hugh, conforming thus to the pious wishes of his father. In 1118 he gave a donation for the support of this priory, to be obtained out of a portion of his rents from some of his lands in Langham, England. M. D'Acy, from whose book the foregoing details have been translated by the author of this pamphlet, remarks on this donation, "One sees by this that the Tyrrells at that time possessed large land holdings in England, and that Walter Tyrrell I. had received his share of the spoils from the Conquest."

Sir Walter Tyrrell III. founded the Monastery of St. Pierre de Sélincourt and the Abbey of St. Larme. This monastery and abbey were pronounced to be the most beautiful in all Picardy, nexft after the great Cathedral at Amiens, and they constituted for many generations the sepulchre of the Tyrrells. They were owned for a number of years by the family of Gédéon de Forceville, of Amiens, but they have been in ruins since the revolution of 1789. .

Hugh Tyrrell I., son of *Sir Walter Tyrrell III.*, inherited the lands and titles of his father and was Lord of Poix, *Vicomte d'Equennes,* etc., and qualified as *Prince de Poix* in 1153, 1155 and 1159. Hugh confirmed the grants of his father to the said churches as above mentioned; he also made one of the Crusades. He married *Ada d'Aumale,* the daughter of *Etienne de Champagne, Comte d'Aumale.* This Ada d'Aumale was lineally descended from *Richard II.,* Duke of Normandy, and from *Ralf de Mortemer,* Baron of Wigmore. Sir Hugh Tyrrell I. made his will in 1158 and died in 1159, leaving among other sons *Walter Tyrrell IV.,* who died in 1171 without children, and *Hugh Tyrrell II.,* who finally succeeded to the titles and possessions of the family. There were also other children, and among them, *Adam Tyrrell,* who became the founder of the *Moyencourt* family. Sir Hugh Tyrrell II. was a great soldier and distinguished himself in the Crusades. In the Hall of the Crusades, in the great palace at Versailles, in Folio 24, No. 125, is an article on *Sir Hugh Tyrrell, Lord of Poix,* and one of the leaders of thc Crusades. His coat of arms is in the third Hall of the Crusades. They are spread upon the beam which is above the picture representing the "Raising of the Siege at Rhodes," August 17, 1480. The escutcheon bears the date of 1147, and is under the name of Hugh Tyrrell, Lord of Poix.

Sir Hugh Tyrrell was accompanied to the Crusades in 1190 by four of his cousins, two of whom perished at the siege of Acre in 1191. Sir Hugh II. died in 1199 and was buried in the Abbey of St. Pierre Sélincourt. He had married, first, in 1161, *Isabelle de Wignacourt,* who was of an illustrious House in Picardy; and second, in 1173, *Marie de Sénarpont,* who was also of distinguished blood.

Sir Walter Tyrrell I. had received from the Conqueror large tracts of land in Hampshire and in Essex. He did not live long after the Conquest, but in 1067, when William I. of England went over into Normandy, *Sir Walter Tyrrell I.* was left as one of his High Commissioners for the County of Essex during his temporary absence. He held the lordship of Laingaham in Essex; was lord of the Manors of Kingsworthy and Avon-Tyrrell in the New Forest; and also held the "Sueburga" and "Contona" in Somerset from Osmond, Bishop of Salisbury. There is some dispute as to the date of the death of *Sir Walter Tyrrell I.,* as the French authority so frequently quoted herein gives it as in 1068, but Mr. Tyrrell in his history of the family gives it as occurring in 1080. As before said, he was succeeded by his grandson, *Sir Walter Tyrrell III.,* his son, *Sir Walter II.,* having pre-deceased him. The wife of Sir Walter Tyrrell III., *Adelaide,* was a cousin of the Conqueror, who had commanded her marriage to Sir Walter, and she appears to have lived to a great age, for according to the Pipe Roll of 1136 she was seized as a widow of the Manor of Langham in Essex. Sir Walter Tyrrell III. joined the first Crusade and was present at the siege of Jerusalem in 1096. It was at this time that he adopted what are known as the "Poix" arms to distinguish himself from his kinsman, the Sire de Tirel, who was also taking part in the siege. Reference to this coat of arms will be made hereafter in this pamphlet. There has been much conflict in the authorities as to just the manner in which King William Rufus met his death, and it has been disputed that the accident was due to Sir Walter Tyrrell III. However, all the authorities agree that it was purely the result of an accident, as Sir Walter and the King were great friends and kinsmen and had for many years been on terms of the greatest intimacy. Late in life lie made another pilgrimage to the Holy Land, and dying in 1135 was succeeded by his son, *Hugh Tyrrell I.,* as before stated, who was the first one of the family to bear the title of *Prince of Poix,* and who is mentioned by the Norman historian, Ordericus, as an ardent soldier. Sir Hugh Tyrrell I. joined the second Crusade of 1146. In the Pipe Roll he is named as being seized of the Manors of Kingsworthy near Winchester, Avon-Tyrrell, and also lands at Ripley, Shirley, and Sopley in the New Forest. This Sir Hugh gave the chateau and lands of Moyencourt to his fourth son, Adam, from whom descends the House of *Tyrrell de Moyencourt,* (which name he then took) , represented in France to this day. As before stated. Sir Hugh Tyrrell I. was ultimately succeeded by his son. *Sir Hugh Tyrrell II.,* who was the sixth Lord of Poix. Sir Hugh Tyrrell II. was conspicuously identified with the first conquest of Ireland by the English and accompanied his cousin, *Strongbow, Earl of Pembroke,* to that country in 1169. He was made Baron of Castleknock in 1173 and was Governor of Trim in 1183. He was at the siege of Acre in the Crusades of 1191 and was known as the "Grecian Knight," Sir Hugh Tyrrell II. was buried at Sélincourt in 1199. He left a number of children. The eldest son, *Sir Walter Tyrrell V.,* succeeded to the titles and possessions of the family in Picardy and Normandy, under the usual law of primogeniture.

Another son of *Sir Hugh II., Richard Tyrrell,* succeeded his father as to the Irish titles and possessions, and became the second Baron of Castleknock. This Richard Tyrrell of Castleknock was the founder of all the different branches of the English-Irish family of Tyrrell. In the history of the family published by Mr. Tyrrell in 1904, all the pedigrees of the descendants of Richard Tyrrell, Baron of Castleknock, are fully given down to the present time, and show that the various descendants, in the many centuries that have elapsed since the family was first established in Ireland, have held numerous titles and positions of honor and have been distinguished in the troublesome periods of Irish history in many ways.

Another son of *Sir Hugh Tyrrell II., Roger Tyrrell* of Hampshire, succeeded to the vast possessions of his father in Hampshire and in Essex, and became the ancestor of all of the English branches of the family.

Before taking up the matter of the several branches in England descended from Roger Tyrrell, it may be interesting to note briefly the subsequent fortunes of the old stock left in France. *Sir Walter Tyrrell V.,* who had succeeded to the vast estates and the many titles of the family in Picardy, Normandy and other parts of France, died in Picardy in 1228, and was succeeded as to these titles and possessions by his oldest son. *Sir Hugh Tyrrell III.,* who was killed in battle in 1272. The latter was succeeded by *Sir William Tyrrell I.,* who died in 1302. Sir William I. was succeeded by his oldest son. *Sir William II.,* who died in 1323. The oldest son of Sir William Tyrrell II., *Sir John I.,* succeeded to the various titles and lands, and was killed at the battle of Crécy on the French side in 1346, when the Black Prince of England won his great victory. He was succeeded by his son, *John II.,* who died in 1361. He in turn was succeeded by *John III.,* who died in 1381. His successor, *John IV.,* was killed in battle in 1402, and he was succeeded by his son, *John V.,* who was Grand Admiral of France, and who, with his relative, *Roques Tyrrell de Poix,* was killed at the battle of Agincourt in 1415. These deaths in this great battle left, as the sole male heir of the titles and landed possessions in France of the family of Tyrrell de Poix, a boy twelve years old, *Philippe,* son of John v., who died two years later in 1417, thus extinguishing the male line in France of the oldest branch Of the family. The titles and landed possessions then went, through the preceding marriage of *Marguerite Tyrrell de Poix* to *Thibaut Soissons,* into the distinguished family of *Moyencourt-Soissons-Morenil,* as hereinbefore stated. *Cardinal Richelieu,* the great Prime Minister of France in the seventeenth century, was descended, through his maternal line in the Moyencourt family, from the old Norman House of Tyrrell de Poix. These data as to the details of the family history in Normandy and Picardy, after the settlement of members of the family in England, have been translated from the elaborate history so frequently referred to herein, published by M. D'Acy in Paris in 1869.

Coming back to *Roger Tyrrell*, son of *Sir Hugh Tyrrell II.*, who, as has been said, became the ancestor of the different branches of the family in England, it may be said that there is some confusion in the authorities as to the first two generations after Sir Roger, relative to his marriage and to the names of his children and grandchildren. It is sufficiently clear, however, and well established that his great-grandson was *Sir Edward Tyrrell*, who married the daughter and heiress of *Sir William Borgate* of Suffolk. Mr. Joseph H. Tyrrell, the English historian of the family, spent many years in the preparation of his book and has devoted much patient investigation to the early history of the various English branches of the family, and he states that it is quite evident that these branches all come from Sir Walter III. and Sir Hugh I. and II., as Sir John Tyrrell of Heron was possessed of the Avon-Tyrrell properties in Hampshire in the seventeenth century. (It will be recalled that Hugh I., son of Walter III., owned these lands in 1159, according to the Pipe Roll.) There is a marginal note on a pedigree by Segar, Garter King of Arms, stating that Sir John Tyrrell of Heron sold this Manor early in the seventeenth century.

Sir Edward Tyrrell, who married the daughter of Sir William Borgate, as above mentioned, left a son. *Sir Hugh Tyrrell*, of Great Thomdon, Essex, who was living in the time of Edward III. of England. He was the Governor of Carisbroke Castle, which he defended against the French in 1378. The son of this Sir Hugh Tyrrell of Essex, *Sir James Tyrrell*, married *Margaret*, the daughter and heiress of *Sir William Heron*, Knight, of Heron in Essex, and thus became the ancestor of practically the entire family of Tyrrell in England, which became known as the *Tyrrells of Heron*. Different members of the Tyrrells of Heron in succeeding generations settled in other counties in England, notably in Buckinghamshire, Oxfordshire and Suffolk. From the above mentioned marriage of Sir James Tyrrell and Margaret of Heron came the several branches of the family in England known as the Tyrrells of Springfield and the Tyrrells of Thornton, to which branches references will hereinafter be made.

Mr. J. H. Tyrrell, in his "History of the Tyrrells," gives the detailed pedigrees, lists of marriages and complete line of descent from Baron Richard Tyrrell, of Castleknock, and Sir Roger Tyrrell of Hampshire, all of the twelfth century, down, with scarcely a missing link in the chain, to the present representatives of the family in Ireland and England. He does not always give the names of all the children born in the successive generations, but does give most of them and the oldest son in each case who inherited the lands and title.

The old coat of arms adopted by *Sir Walter Tyrrell III.,* known as the "Poix" arms, is carefully described in heraldic language, with an illustration of its appearance, in the elaborate publication of M. D'Acy. This was the coat of arms selected by Sir Walter to distinguish his bearings from the arms of his elder kinsman, the *Sire de Tirel,* who took part with him also at the siege of Acre in 1096, during the first Crusade.

Armorial bearings were probably assumed by *Ralf, Sire de Tirel,* about the year 970 A. D., for the device of his oldest son, Hilduin, was a shield "Vair." This word "Vair" is used in heraldic language to indicate the different tinctures or colors and their method of arrangement on the shield, the word itself indicating a peculiar kind of fur which was largely in use about the tenth century. *Sir Walter Tyrrell I.,* who came to England with the Conqueror, also bore "Vair" on his shield, as did his son and grandson. The arms of Poix, assumed by *Sir Walter Tyrrell III.,* at the siege of Jerusalem, were as follows: Gules, with bend argent, together with six crosses, recrossed with small crosslets and pointed in gold, posed three and three. M. D'Acy, referring to the coat of arms of the family of Tyrrell de Poix, says, "It is in this manner that this coat of arms is represented painted in the historic museum at Versailles in the third hall of the Crusades." The swords on it, with crosses recrossed, were evidently symbolic of the fact that the prominent members of the family in Picardy had taken distinguished parts in the Crusades. After this, changes seem to have been made in some features, for *Sir Hugh Tyrrell II.,* born about 1130, bore "Vair, on a chief gules, a demi-lion rampant, or," and on succeeding to the titles and possessions of Poix in 1171 he became entitled to bear also the "Poix" arms. Some time after the conquest of Ireland by the English under Strongbow, the following arms were adopted either by *Hugh Tyrrell II.* or by some of his descendants in Ireland: "Gules two bars ermine, between seven crosses pattées or, three, three, and one; on a chief argent a demi-lion rampant gules." (Harleian MSS. 4036.) The motto used by the descendants of Hugh Tyrrell in Ireland probably dates from the year 1100 and consisted of the old Latin motto used in Picardy, "Veritas Via Vitae."

It would seem that *Roger Tyrrell* of Hampshire, the son of *Hugh Tyrrell II.,* who inherited all of the possessions of the latter in Hampshire and Essex, and his descendants never used the old "Poix" arms nor the old motto in Latin above given. Very early in the establishment of the family in England, the coat of arms seems to have been taken which has ever since been identified with the Tyrrells of Heron and the different branches of the family descended from them. This coat of arms goes back into the twelfth or thirteenth century and consisted of the arms in silver, within a bordure engrailed, gules, two chevrons, azure; with the motto, "Sans Dieu Rien;" and with a crest of a peacock's tail issuing from the mouth of a boar's head, couped, erect. This is the coat of arms of which an illustration appears at the head of this little pamphlet. In the pamphlet issued two years ago by the author there was a mistake in the motto given connected with the coat of arms. It there appears as "Sans Crainte." This, the author has learned, is an error, as the motto, "Sans Crainte" belongs exclusively to that branch of the Tyrrells of Heron known as the Tyrrells of Boreham House in Essex, who are the descendants of *John Tyrrell* of Billericay in Essex, and who are still represented in England by *Colonel John Tufnell-Tyrrell,* of

Boreham House, Essex. This motto, "Sans Crainte," was originally that of the *Highams of Boreham*, whose daughter and heiress married *John Tyrrell* of that branch of the family, and in this way that motto became connected with the old coat of arms of the Tyrrells of Heron, but applicable only to that particular branch of the family. The old motto, "Sans Dieu Rien," is that of the Essex Tyrrells and is the only one which any of the American descendants of the Tyrrells of Heron would have the right to use; and this is for the reason also that the motto of "Sans Crainte" was placed on the coat of arms of the Boreham House Tyrrells after the first Virginia ancestor had left England.

The Standard of the *Tyrrells of Heron* was "The Cross of St. George, azure, on a wreath argent and gules, a boar's head couped and erect argent; and issuing from the mouth a peacock's tail. The other charges consisted of six repetitions of the Badge." The Badge of the Tyrrells of Heron was "Three long bows fretted in triangle," which afterwards took the form of a continuous knot. The descriptions of the Standards and Badges are from the MSS. of Sir Christopher Barker, Garter King of Arms, who died in 1549. (Harleian MSS. 4633 and "Excerpta Historica".)

The pennon of the Tyrrells was the Badge on a triangular flag gules.

A very interesting description of the arms of the *Tirrell-Tyrrell* family, told in heraldic language, will be found in a very rare book in the Virginia State Library at Richmond, called the "Visitations of Essex," part 1, page 299. The description here given will show how the early generations of the family in England gradually built up their coat of arms from the original shield of the Tyrrells of Heron by additions taken from probably the coats of arms respectively of the different families into which the earliest members of the family had married, such as the *Borgates*, the *Coggeshalls*, the *Swynfords*, the *Flamberts*, etc.

In this same book of the "Visitations" there will be found very interesting lists in quaint and old-fashioned spelling of the pedigrees of the different English branches from the time of *Sir Walter Tyrrell III.* in England down to about the year 1550.

In speaking of the coat of arms that decorates one of the title pages of this little pamphlet, it may be stated incidentally that the tiger supporters would not be permissible now in England, as supporters are never used in England except when there is an actual existing title to be supported, and as all the titles in the Tyrrell family, such as Baronetcies, etc., have long since become extinct in England. The author has simply given the tigers in the illustration as having at one time formed part of the ancient coat of arms of the Tyrrells of Heron.

Much valuable information as to the English branches of the family may be found in Burke's "Extinct and Dormant Baronetcies," a book easily found in the old book shops in England and possibly in some of the book stores of Boston and New York. Pages 536, 537, 538 and 539 in that book are devoted to the lineage of the Tyrrell family, from its first establishment in England by *Sir Walter Tyrrell III.* down to a late period in the eighteenth century. Burke remarks: "The family of Tirrell is one of great note and antiquity, and for more than 600 years its Chief, in a direct line, enjoyed the honor of Knighthood." In the long list of pedigrees in this book it will be noticed that the same differences exist in the manner of spelling the surname that have been mentioned in M. D'Acy's book and also in the history of the family prepared by Mr. Tyrrell. In Burke's list the name is frequently spelled Tirrell, Tyrrell, etc., and frequently the surname of the son is spelled differently from that of the father. All this goes to show that these different spellings were of one and the same family name, and that like many other old family surnames in England there have been many changes in the form of spelling from one generation to another. In Burke's list of the first five or six generations from *Sir Walter Tyrrell III.* down to *Sir Edward Tyrrell,* who married the Suffolk heiress by the name of *Borgate,* he makes a number of errors, stating that the ancestor was succeeded in a direct line by, first, his son. *Sir Henry Tyrrell;* and the latter by *Sir*

Richard; and he by *Sir Edward;* and he by *Sir Geofrey;* and he by *Sir Lionel,* etc., down to Sir Edward. In the more accurately prepared lists given in Mr. Tyrrell's elaborate history of the family, this is all shown to be an error, and the true descent was as follows: *Sir Walter Tyrrell III.* was succeeded by his son. *Sir Hugh I.,* and he by *Sir Hugh II., Prince of Poix,* who was the ancestor who permanently established the family both in England and Ireland and who took part in the conquest of Ireland and in the Crusades. On the death of Sir Hugh II., his body was taken and deposited in the old mausoleum of the family in Picardy at Sélincourt. He was succeeded in his titles and possessions in France, as has before been said, by his oldest son, *Walter Tyrrell V.* Another son, *Richard,* who was the second Baron of Castleknock, became the founder of the Irish branches of the family, and another son of Hugh II., *Roger Tyrrell* of Hampshire, who was a son by the second marriage with *Marie de Sénarpont,* inherited his lands and possessions in England and became the founder of all the English branches of the family. Sir Roger Tyrrell was succeeded by his son. *Sir Edward,* and he by his son. *Sir Galfrid,* and the son of Sir Galfrid was the *Sir Edward Tyrrell* who married *Jane* or *Joan,* the daughter and heiress of *Sir William Borgate.* The earlier members of the family in England, such as Sir Walter III., Sir Hugh I. and Sir Hugh II., spent much of their time still in France, living at times in their various chateaux in Picardy, and were still, to all intents and purposes, noblemen of Picardy as well as Barons in England. Sir Walter Tyrrell III., while living in one of his castles in Picardy, was visited there by Anselm, Archbishop of Canterbury.

There is another error which is frequently met with in statements as to the prominent members of the Tyrrell family in early days, and that is, that the *Chevalier Bayard du Terrail,* the Knight "sans peur et sans reproche," was a distinguished member of the family. This statement is not true. The family name, or surname, of the Chevalier was Bayard, just as Tyrrell is the surname of the family in question. The affix, "du Terrail," was not a surname at all, but was simply an indication as to the locality from which the Chevalier's family came. The name Terrail in French means "pottery works," and is pronounced in French, as nearly as it can be expressed in English, "Terrye." This family was a Burgundian family from the eastern borders of France, and the gallant Chevalier was born in that province of Burgundy known as Dauphiné, and his family became entirely extinct a few generations after his death. This family of Bayard du Terrail had no connection whatever with the family of Tyrrell de Poix of Normandy and Picardy.

During the investigations of the author of this pamphlet in the British Museum Library, he came across an interesting little brochure, published by Mr. Peter G. Laurie, called "The Tyrells of Heron, in the Parish of East Horndon." The author found this to be an exceedingly interesting account of the County family of the Tyrrells which had been settled in Essex for over 500 years on lands probably originally granted during the time of, or shortly after, the Conquest. These Tyrrells of Heron were descendants of *Sir Roger Tyrrell* of Hampshire, and their Manor House located near East Homdon was occupied by the family for a number of centuries, down to a period early in the seventeenth century, when *Sir John Tyrrell*, who was born in 1571, sold this Manor House and its lands, known as Heron Hall, and went to live at Springfield near Chelmsford in Essex County. The author read this pamphlet with great interest and opened up a correspondence from London with Mr. Laurie, who was temporarily occupying his beautiful country seat near East Horndon in Essex, known as "Heroncourt," Herongate, near Brentwood, Essex. The result of this correspondence was that Mr. Laurie invited the author of this pamphlet and his wife to visit the place near his country seat, where the old Tyrrell Manor House, known as Heron Hall, had been located, and near which Was the old Tyrrell Chapel, in which were buried many members of the family back to the thirteenth century. Mr. Laurie kindly put himself at the service of the author and offered to accompany the party when the locality should be visited and to show the spots of interest in that neighborhood, inviting them afterwards most courteously to take tea under the shade of his beautiful oaks, where an American descendant of this old Essex County family could have the opportunity of meeting the members of his family. So, in August, 1906, the author and his wife went down to the little station of Brentwood, on the main line of the Great Eastern Railway, about twenty miles northeast of London. Driving out to Mr. Laurie's place, the party met the courteous and scholarly gentleman, who rode with them to visit Tyrrell Chapel, located about a mile from his country seat. East Horndon is a village and parish on the road from Brentwood to Orsett and is about three miles south from Brentwood railway station and about twenty-two miles from London. The little church visited is cabled the Church of All Saints, and is an edifice of red brick, erected about the time of Henry V., and consists of a chancel and a large aisle on the south called the Tyrrell Chapel, and a smaller chapel on the north, a nave, transepts, south porch, and a massive but somewhat stunted tower at the west end containing four bells, the lower stage of which tower is used as a vestry. In the chancel floor is an interesting slab with inscription: "To Sir Thomas Tyrrell, son and heir of Sir John Tyrrell, Knight, and Alice, his wife," dated 1422. There are also monuments in the north and south chapels to other members of the family buried in the vaults below at different periods, among others. Sir John Tyrrell, died 1675, and Dame Martha, his wife, died 1670. The chancel referred to is enriched with handsomely carved bosses. Against the south transept there is an altar tomb, said to be a memorial of the burial here of the heart of Queen Anne Boleyn, who was beheaded May 19, 1536. The chapel on the north side is called the Marney Chapel; the name, Mamey, came from the marriage, in the early part of the sixteenth century, of *Sir Thomas Tyrrell* of Heron to *Anna,* daughter of *Sir John Marney,* Knight, of Essex. High upon the wall of the old church in the interior, was fastened an ancient helmet, said to be part of the armor of old *Sir John Tyrrell,* who fought at the battle of Agincourt under Henry V. in 1415. The helmet has been placed in the church for many hundred years. Fastened to the top of the helmet, in bronze, was the crest of the Tyrrell family, the boar's head with the peacock's tail issuing from the mouth, towering above the helmet six or eight inches; as one might say, like the plume of Henry of Navarre. The helmet was battered here and there with dents received by the doughty old knight in battle. Also nailed up along side the helmet were the bronze jointed gauntlets of the old mediaeval hero. These relics of the church are carefully guarded and are held very sacred. In the vaults under the chapel were buried *Sir James Tyrrell* of Heron, 1476; *Sir John Tyrrell,* who distinguished himself in the Civil War in the time of Cromwell on the side of the King; *Sir Charles, Sir Edward,* and other members of the family. There was also a highly prized alabaster slab tablet to the memory of *Lady Alice Tyrrell,* upon which were outlined her figure and face, placed in the church in 1422, seventy years before America was discovered. This was Lady Alice, daughter of *Sir William Coggeshall* and wife of *Sir John Tyrrell,* of Agincourt fame. The mother of this Lady Alice Tyrrell was *Antiocha,* who was the daughter of the famous English soldier. *Sir John Hawkwood,* Knight, of Essex, who for many years, during the wars between the Guelphs and Ghibellines in Italy, was the commanding general of the armies of Florence. A magnificent portrait of him was seen by the author of this pamphlet in 1906 hanging in the Duomo or Cathedral at Florence, Italy. The little church at East Horndon is now undergoing restoration, and all of these relics are most carefully preserved and protected. A rectory house was built in 1877 at the village of Herongate. The village is about three-quarters of a mile north of the church. About a mile from the old chapel and about a quarter of a mile from the village of Herongate is the site of the old Manor House of Heron Hall, the home of the Tyrrells of Heron for over five hundred years. Heron Hall was built in the thirteenth or fourteenth century. It was an imposing edifice constructed of brick, with a large central quadrangular court, and an extensive terrace on the east side, and was entirely surrounded by a moat. At each of the four corners stood massive round towers. The old building was destroyed about a hundred years ago or more, and no trace of it can now be seen; but the old moat which surrounded the Hall is still in existence and contains water; a small portion of the old garden wall is also still to be seen. The Hall was located on a noble site, commanding a view of twenty miles of the valley of the Thames and the hills of Kent on the other side of the river. The plan of old Heron Hall, as it formerly existed, made in 1788, may still be seen at the residence of Mr. Laurie, known as Heroncourt. Mr. Laurie himself is a vestryman in the old church, and being of antiquarian tastes and having lived in this part of Essex County for many years, he prepared his pamphlet on this old Essex County family on account of the local interest attaching to it. As he explained to the author on this visit, it was a family which dominated this portion of England for many centuries, and its members held the very highest positions in the County. That particular local branch living in this part of the County had died out in the latter part of the eighteenth century, when its last member, the *Countess of Arran,* died.

During this same month of August, 1906, the author of this pamphlet visited the old University town of Oxford, and, in looking over the Alumni registers of that University, he found that *Sir Timothy Tyrrell* of Oakley in Bucks, as well as his son. *Sir Timothy II.,* were both graduates of the University of Oxford. These members of the family are referred to in Evelyn's Diary as living in a beautiful country seat near Oxford, called Shotover, (from the French, Chateau Vert). The name of this Sir Timothy Tyrrell will be found in Burke's book above referred to in these notes, on page 538 in a foot note. It has generally been considered in the traditions of the Virginia Tyrrells that the first Virginia ancestor was a descendant of this Sir Timothy Tyrrell of Oakley in Bucks. The date, of the arrival of the first members of the Tyrrell family in Virginia seems to be involved in some obscurity. It is a tradition that a *Thomas Terrell* (or *Tyrrell*) arrived in Virginia about 1637, and a *James Tyrrell* in 1648, but nothing has ever been learned as to these two immigrants, or as to any descendants from them. It is known, however, that *Richmond* and *William Tyrrell,* or *Terrell,* arrived in Virginia from England about the middle of the seventeenth century. The author of this pamphlet is a lineal descendant in direct line from William Terrell, one of these first two immigrants, and the line of his descent from this ancestor will be given hereinafter. In the old colonial land records at Richmond, Va., in the first mention made of William's arrival and his connection with lands, his surname is spelled "Tyrrell." In the same records, where the first mention is made of his brother Richmond, the name of the latter is spelled "Tirrell." There is a deed referred to in the William and Mary Quarterly, Volume 13, page 264, whereby Richmond Terrell conveys to Henry Wyatt a tract of land in New Kent County, Va. The date of the deed is April 29, 1670, and in it the grantor reserves 100 acres, which he says he had previously given unto his brother William Terrell, and which has since been sold by the latter to Francis Waring. This deed clearly shows that Richmond and William were brothers.

The traditions among the descendants of William and Richmond Terrell are sometimes contradictory as to just where in England the two brothers came from, and as to the exact year of their arrival. They are all in accord, however, in saying that the two came from the old family of the Tyrrells in England and were descendants of the stock established there by Sir Walter Tyrrell III. As before stated, the tradition generally relied upon is that *William* and *Richmond* were the sons of *William Tyrrell,* who was the son of *Sir Timothy Tyrrell I.* of Oakley. This *Sir Timothy Tyrrell* was the son of *Sir Edward Tyrrell* of Thornton and belonged to that branch of the English family known as the Tyrrells of Thornton, who were an offshoot of the Tyrrells of Heron. This William Tyrrell, son of Sir Timothy Tyrrell I., was killed at the battle of Chester in 1644, during the Civil War in England. Richmond and William Terrell were both large land owners in Virginia at a very early period after their arrival. The family traditions are that they came to Virginia with some sort of official authority in connection with the crown lands in Virginia, either as surveyors or in some other important capacity. It has generally been supposed that the large grants of land received by both of these immigrants came for their services in connection with their official position. It is a significant fact that the Christian name of *Timothy* was largely used in the first two or three generations of the descendants of both *Richmond* and *William,* and that among the children of *William* were five who bore the exact Christian names of five of the children and grandchildren of Sir Timothy Tyrrell of Oakley in Bucks. As to whether these two Virginia colonists, Richmond and William Terrell, were lineally descended from Sir Timothy Tyrrell I., or from Sir Edward of Thornton, is not yet quite clearly established in the mind of the author of this pamphlet; but that they came from the old stock of the Tyrrells of Heron, and probably the Tyrrells of Thornton, is substantially established in many ways. Among the descendants of William now living in the State of Georgia, there is an old gold watch, said to have been brought over by William from England, and still held in the family as a valuable relic, which has engraved upon it the old crest of the Tyrrells of Heron, namely, the crest of the boar's head with the peacock's tail issuing therefrom. Moreover, there is another branch of the family in Virginia an old ring, handed down from many generations back in that State, with the same crest engraved thereon.

Sir Timothy Tyrrell I. of Oakley was the son of Sir Edward Tyrrell of Thornton, as before stated, and a descendant of the Tyrrells of Heron, and was born in 1575. In the correspondence which the author has had for a year past with Mr. J. H. Tyrrell, the English historian of the family, Mr. Tyrrell has intimated that the Virginia ancestor of the family probably came from the branch known in England as the Tyrrells of Thornton. In a letter dated June 9, 1908, from Mr. Tyrrell to the author, giving his views on this subject, he says among other things, "It may interest you to know that no matter from what branch of the English house the American families come, they are of Royal descent, as you will see by the enclosed chart, which do not trouble yourself to return to me." Included in this letter was a very elaborate chart, carefully prepared by Mr. Tyrrell from the authorities so accessible in England, showing the line of descent from *Edward I., King of England,* and *Eleanor of Castile,* his wife, to *Sir Edward Tyrrell* of Thornton, through the marriage of *Joan Plantagenet,* the daughter of *Edward I.,* to *Gilbert de Clare, Earl of Gloucester.* Joan Plantagenet is sometimes called in history Joan of Acre, as she was born during the siege of Acre in the Crusades, where Edward I., then Prince of Wales, was taking part, accompanied by Eleanor of Castile, his wife.

There are doubtless many families in America who are descended from Royal ancestors, but it is not always easy to establish this fact by accurate lists of the marriages and pedigrees.

In a Republic like that of the United States, where transcendent genius, relying upon character, industry and opportunity, can enable a man to rise from the depths of poverty and obscurity to the loftiest station of usefulness, honor and fame, like the immortal Abraham Lincoln, descent from Royalty, no matter how regular and honorable, seems of trivial importance indeed. In many cases, the character of a Sovereign has been so disreputable or vicious that to have him as an ancestor would be anything but creditable. However, as Edward Plantagenet (Edward I. of England), was a great law giver, soldier and statesman, and probably the ablest King that England ever had, one whose strong personality, keen intelligence and vigorous character were deeply impressed upon English history, it may possibly be a matter of curious genealogical interest for descendants of this old English County family to read the line of descent so carefully prepared by Mr. Tyrrell, showing the lineage of the Tyrrells of Thornton from the Plantagenet King. Therefore, the author will here insert the chart which was sent to him as above described.

Royal Descent of English Branch of Tyrrell, from the Two Marriages of Joan Plantagenet.

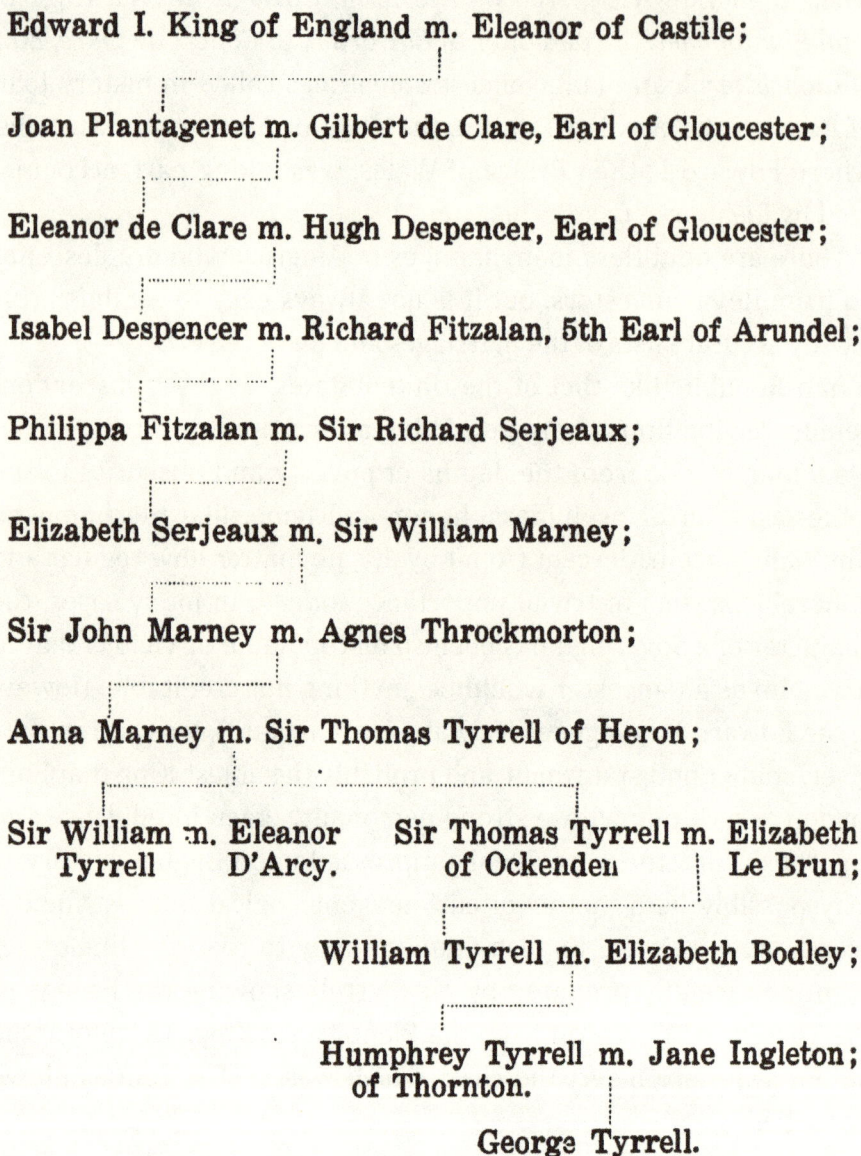

Edward I. King of England m. Eleanor of Castile;

Joan Plantagenet m. Gilbert de Clare, Earl of Gloucester;

Eleanor de Clare m. Hugh Despencer, Earl of Gloucester;

Isabel Despencer m. Richard Fitzalan, 5th Earl of Arundel;

Philippa Fitzalan m. Sir Richard Serjeaux;

Elizabeth Serjeaux m. Sir William Marney;

Sir John Marney m. Agnes Throckmorton;

Anna Marney m. Sir Thomas Tyrrell of Heron;

Sir William m. Eleanor   Sir Thomas Tyrrell m. Elizabeth
Tyrrell   D'Arcy.   of Ockenden   Le Brun;

William Tyrrell m. Elizabeth Bodley;

Humphrey Tyrrell m. Jane Ingleton;
of Thornton.

George Tyrrell.

After the death of Joan's first husband, the Earl of Gloucester, she married a second time, her second husband being *Ralf de Monthermer*. The line of descent from this second marriage was as follows:

Her son, Sir Thomas Monthermer m. Margaret ————;

Margaret Monthermer m. Sir John de Montacute;

Sir Simon Montacute m. Elizabeth Boughton;

Thomas Montagu m. Christian Bassett;

John Montagu m. Alice Halcot;

William Montagu m. Mary Butline;

Richard Montagu m. Agnes Knotting;

Thomas Montagu m. Agnes Dudley;

Sir Edward Montagu, Chief Justice, m. Helen Roper;

Eleanor Montagu.

George Tyrrell, who was descended from the first marriage of Joan Plantagenet, married *Eleanor Montagu,* who was descended from the second marriage of Joan. Their oldest son was *Sir Edward Tyrrell* of Thornton, who married, first, *Mary Lee,* and, second, *Margaret Aston.* From the first marriage Sir Edward had a son. *Sir Edward Tyrrell,* Baronet, of Thornton, who married *Elizabeth Kingsmill,* daughter of *Sir William Kingsmill,* who was also of Royal descent. By the second marriage of Sir Edward Tyrrell of Thornton he had a son. *Sir Timothy Tyrrell I.* of Oakley in Bucks, who married

Eleanor Kingsmill, also a daughter of *Sir William Kingsmill.* From this chart it will easily be seen that there were three branches of the family, all of which were descended from Joan Plantagenet, namely, the branch headed by Sir William Tyrrell, who married Eleanor D'Arcy, and the two branches headed respectively by Sir Edward Tyrrell, Baronet, and Sir Timothy I. of Oakley.

Sir Timothy Tyrrell I. was Master of the Buckhounds to King James I. and King Charles I. He was succeeded in his title by his oldest son. *Sir Timothy Tyrrell II.,* who was of Oakley in Bucks, and also of Shotover in the County of Oxford. The latter was also of the Privy Chamber of King Charles I.; he was Colonel in the Royal Army, Governor of Cardiff, and General of the Ordnance. One of his sons, *James Tyrrell,* was a historian of some distinction, having written a general history of England in five volumes. In M. D'Acy's book, referred to in the foregoing part of these notes, he speaks of the historian, James Tyrrell, as a descendant of the old Norman-French family of Tyrrell de Poix, and mentions the fact that this James Tyrrell had written considerably on the subject of the old family in France.

As to the place in England from which Richmond and William Terrell came, there is much obscurity, owing to the absence of documentary evidence on that point and to the long period that has elapsed, about two hundred and fifty years, since they came to the colony. One tradition is that they came directly from Richmond, England; and it is somewhat significant in this connection that the residence of Sir Timothy Tyrrell I., while he was an official member of the household of King Charles I., must have been in the neighborhood of Richmond, as the residence of the Stuart Kings was at Hampton Court nearby. It has been insisted by some that the first Tyrrells in Virginia came from England via the West Indies. It is known that Usher Tyrrell, one of the sons of Sir Timothy II., located himself in Jamaica. He had married a daughter of Van Tromp, the Dutch Admiral, and had children. At that early date the route via the West Indies was frequently taken by the colonial immigrants.

Bristol, on the west coast of England, was quite accessible to the Tyrrells in Oxford and Bucks; and equally so, probably, was the route down the Thames, which would also be convenient to any member of the old stock left still in Essex, as Langham, Ramsey-Tyrrells, Boreham House, Springfield, Thornton, Heron Hall, and other places in Essex, where the Tyrrells had lived and flourished in the thirteenth, fourteenth and fifteenth centuries, were all within a short distance of that river. The Civil Wars in England caused the emigration of many members of the old cavalier families, especially the younger sons who could not inherit under the laws of primo-geniture, to the colony of Virginia. The Tyrrells had largely taken the losing side in the conflict, and some of the more adventurous spirits among the younger members of the family evidently desired to shake the dust of England from their feet and seek their fortunes in the new world. William and Richmond may not have left England until after the Restoration of Charles II., although Richmond is said to have arrived as early as 1656.

Therefore, being members of a family which had been loyal to King Charles I. in his great contest with Parliament, they may have obtained under the Restoration from Charles II. some authoritative position with reference to the crown lands or Royal hunting grounds in the colony of Virginia. Reference has been made herein already to the tradition in the family that the first ancestors came out from England under some such Royal authority.

The Tyrrell family in Ireland has produced many men of great distinction in the history of that country. Many were conspicuous in the wars that have devastated Ireland, and a number who have headed the different branches of the family in that country have borne the title of Baron and have been distinguished as owners of imposing castles and large possessions of lands. Many of these Irish Tyrrells were graduates of Trinity College, Dublin, and occupied many high positions in connection with the Corporation of that city.

All along through the pages of English history from the thirteenth century down, the members of the family have been distinguished for patriotic and conspicuous service to their country. *Sir John Tyrrell* fought with the Black Prince in 1356 at the battle of Poitiers. Reference has already been made to the presence of old *Sir John Tyrrell,* High Sheriff of Essex, at the battle of Agincourt in 1415. *Sir William Tirrell* was killed at the battle of Barnett in 1471, fighting desperately at the side of Warwick, the King Maker. Another *Sir William Tyrrell* was executed during the Wars of the Roses as a Lancastrian in 1461. The only member of the family, in these early days, who seems to have disgraced the family, was *Sir James Tyrrell*, who was a supporter of Richard III., and who has been charged with having caused the murder of the two sons of Edward IV. in the Tower of London, at the behest of his Sovereign. This Sir James was a son of *Sir William Tyrrell* of Gipping in Suffolk, who was a descendant of the Tyrrells of Heron. During the great Civil War in England between Parliament and Charles I., many members of the family, as has been said, were distinguished for loyal services, mainly in the Royal army. Notably among them was *Sir John Tyrrell;* whose wife was *Martha,* daughter of *Sir Laurence Washington* of Wiltshire, who was of the same family as the illustrious George Washington. These are the "Sir John" and "Dame Martha" hereinbefore referred to as being buried in Tyrrell Chapel. *Sir Thomas Tyrrell,* Judge of the Common Pleas, was one of the Commissioners of the Great Seal to Oliver Cromwell, and seems to have been one of the few of the family who were on the side of Parliament. *Sir John Tyssen Tyrrell* of Boreham House, near Chelmsford in Essex, a descendant of Sir Thomas Tyrrell of Heron, died in 1877. The representative of this branch of the family now in England is Colonel John Tufnell-Tyrrell. There is a tablet in Westminster Abbey to the memory of *Richard Tyrrell,* who was a distinguished Admiral in the naval service of England in the eighteenth century and was a member of one of the Irish branches of the family. All the evidence points to the fact that the family was what is known in England as an old County family, the members of which were always prompt to go to the front when duty called. The position of High Sheriff of

Essex County, which in England is a position of great note and dignity, was held for many years by different members of the family. *Old Sir John Tyrrell,* who fought at Agincourt, was repeatedly elected Speaker of the House of Commons in the fifteenth century. *Sir Timothy Tyrrell II.* was famous for his princely hospitality at his beautiful country place six miles from the city of Oxford. Everyone who is descended from this old historic family may feel proud of the fact that it was a representative of good Norman-English stock; and that in the various positions which its members occupied in the civil and military history of their country, they generally and uniformly conferred high credit upon the family. They never seem to have forgotten that their forefathers had been leaders of men, prominent in the early history of France and taking conspicuous parts in the Crusades.

In concluding these notes, the author of this sketch desires to give his own line of descent from his Virginia ancestors. He has been a resident of San Antonio, Texas, for over thirty years, and is a native of Indiana. His father was Williamson Terrell, who was born in Clark County, Kentucky, June 12, 1805; his mother was Martha Jarrell, who was born in Frankfort, Kentucky, in 1808. She was the daughter of James Jarrell and Rachel Powell, his wife, who both came to Kentucky from Dover, Delaware. Williamson Terrell was the son of Captain John Terrell, who distinguished himself in the early Indian campaigns in the West, under Harmar, St. Clair and Wayne, and who was present at Harmar's defeat and at Wayne's great victory over the Miami Indians at the battle of the Maumee Rapids, or "Fallen Timbers," August 20, 1794. The author's grandfather. Captain John Terrell, was born in Spotsylvania County, Virginia, April 3, 1772, and moved to Kentucky with his father in 1787. John Terrell married Abigail Allan, the author's grandmother, who was the daughter of Archibald Allan of Albemarle County, Virginia, and who was the sister of Chilton Allan, the famous Kentucky lawyer, who represented the Ashland district in Congress for ten years after Henry Clay had been sent to the Senate. The writer's great-grandfather was Henry Terrell, Henry Terrell II., as he is called in the family, to distinguish him from his own father, who was also named Henry. Henry Terrell II. was born in Caroline County, Virginia, March 29, 1735. He married Mary Tyler, who was the daughter of Captain William Tyler, and who was born in Virginia in 1743. The father of Henry Terrell II. was Henry Terrell I., as he is called, who was a lawyer and wealthy planter and who lived near Golansville, in Caroline County, but who was born in Hanover County, Virginia. Henry Terrell I. was born about the year 1695 and died in 1760. A copy of his will is in the possession of his descendant, Colonel Lynch M. Terrell of Atlanta, Ga., together with a copy of the inventory of his estate; and they show that he was a man of large wealth, as property values went at that early day in the colony. He left large, improved tracts of land to each of his several sons, and disposed in his will of a large amount of personal property. Henry Terrell I. was a man of considerable influence in the colony; as was quite common in that day, he combined several occupations and was a lawyer, a merchant and a planter. He made large shipments of goods for the use of his plantations from the port of Bristol in England, and he exported the surplus products of his land, being a large producer especially of tobacco. He was somewhat proud of his family lineage; lived in the comfortable style of a country gentleman, and was rather aristocratic in his ways and bearing. He was married twice; first, to Annie Chiles, a young lady of a family then quite well known and distinguished in the early colonial history of Virginia, several members of that family having been members of the House of Burgesses, and one a Lieutenant Colonel of Virginia Militia. Secondly, Henry Terrell I. married Sarah Woodson, the daughter of Tarlton Woodson. The great-grandfather of the writer of this pamphlet, Henry Terrell II., was a son by the first marriage with Annie Chiles. Henry Terrell I. was one of the younger sons of the Virginia ancestor, William Tyrrell or Terrell, (as the name is written both ways in the early colonial land records). The wife of William Terrell was Susannah Waters; and the tradition in the family is that Susannah came from England to America to meet and marry her husband, William, accompanied by a retinue of servants and escorted by her husband's brother. There is even a romantic story connected with their marriage. It is said that the family of William in England was Catholic, but that while he was a student at the University of Oxford he became a Protestant, thus deeply angering his family; that he had courted Susannah, who was also of Catholic family, many of the old English families still being adherents of that faith at that time. William went to the Virginia colony thus somewhat under his family's displeasure; he was followed later on by Susannah, escorted, as above stated, by his brother; and the marriage took place in Virginia. Of course this is all tradition and it cannot be stated to have any very solid foundation.

The oldest son of William and Susannah Terrell was named Timothy, and the descendants of this son Timothy are quite numerous today in Indiana, Missouri and Colorado. As before stated, it is rather significant that for several generations there was always a Timothy among the descendants of both William and Richmond. There was one daughter of the marriage of William and Susannah whose name was Anna, and who married David Lewis, from which marriage there are many descendants among the oldest families in the State of Virginia. Another son of William and Susannah was David Terrell, who married Agatha Chiles, a sister of the Annie Chiles who had married his brother, Henry Terrell I. From this marriage of David Terrell and Agatha Chiles are descended numerous branches of the family in Texas and other southern states; and among David's descendants is the Hon. A. W. Terrell, of Austin, Texas, now in his eighty-second year, and still a man of great physical and intellectual vigor, who has been prominently identified with the history of Texas for nearly sixty years, and who was the American Minister to Turkey during the last administration of President Cleveland. Among the descendants of another son of William, the ancestor, Joel, is the Hon. Joseph M. Terrell, lately Governor of Georgia; and there are also many descendants of this son still living in that State. There are also many descendants in Virginia and other southern states of Richmond, the brother of William, and one of the first two ancestors in Virginia. William Terrell, the ancestor, lived in St. Paul's Parish, Hanover County, Virginia, and he and his wife, Susannah, were both members of the established church, (Episcopal). This fact may lend some color of truth to the story of their both having recanted from the Catholic faith in England. There is a deed on record in Virginia from William and Susannah Terrell to their son, Henry Terrell, dated March 16, 1725, for a tract of 400 acres of land situated in King William County. William Terrell, the ancestor in Virginia, died at a very advanced age in 1727.

The writer of this little pamphlet has never specially interested himself in tracing down the various branches of the American Terrells from their original Virginia ancestors, and has no special knowledge on this subject further than that of knowing his own direct descent from William Terrell. Other members of the family, notably two cousins of the author, the late General W. H. H. Terrell, of Indianapolis, and his brother. Colonel Lynch M. Terrell, of Atlanta, Ga., have most industriously and thoroughly engaged during the last twenty years in accumulating a vast amount of information on the different branches of the family, descended from the two Virginia ancestors. The author of this sketch has only sought to investigate carefully the early history of the Norman-French progenitors of the stock and the English forefathers, and to trace the direct connection between the first Virginia ancestors and the particular branch of the Tyrrells of Heron from which they undoubtedly came. This work has been done from time to time, in the leisure moments of a busy professional life; and if the results of his researches as set forth in this pamphlet shall prove to be interesting to the many members of the family throughout the United States, the author will be amply compensated for his labors. He desires, in concluding these notes, to express in this public manner, the deep sense of obligation he feels to Mr. Joseph Henry Tyrrell, the English historian of the family, for the kind consideration he has received at his hands and for the many extremely valuable suggestions he has made from time to time by way of aid to the author in his researches and in the preparation of this little pamphlet.

The descendants of this old Essex County family, thus transplanted to Virginia soil some two hundred and fifty years ago, have worthily maintained in America the sturdy and patriotic qualities characteristic of their stock in the mother country. As governors, senators, judges, and other prominent officers in the civil administration of their state and nation, they have taken their full share of honors and credit. In the wars on the borders of Virginia in colonial days; at Guilford Court House, King's Mountain and Yorktown in the Revolution; in the Indian campaigns in the West under Harmar, Wayne and Harrison; at Talladega, the Horseshoe Bend and New Orleans under the indomitable Jackson; at Shiloh, Perryville, Cedar Creek, Cold Harbor, and on many other desperate battle fields of the late Civil War, both in the Federal and Confederate armies, the American descendants of the old Norman-French family of *Tyrrell de Poix* have nobly sustained with their courage and blood the chivalric record established by their knightly forefathers at the siege of Acre in the Crusades, and at Crécy, Poitiers and Agincourt.

9 781789 875539